A Small-Town Summer

by Kristin Cashore
illustrated by Bradley Clark

Scott Foresman
is an imprint of

Glenview, Illinois • Boston, Massachusetts • Chandler, Arizona
Upper Saddle River, New Jersey

Every effort has been made to secure permission and provide appropriate credit for photographic material. The publisher deeply regrets any omission and pledges to correct errors called to its attention in subsequent editions.

Unless otherwise acknowledged, all photographs are the property of Scott Foresman, a division of Pearson Education.

Illustrations by Bradley Clark

Photograph 30 AP/Wide World Photos

ISBN 13: 978-0-328-52668-0
ISBN 10:   0-328-52668-1

Copyright © by Pearson Education, Inc., or its affiliates. All rights reserved.
Printed in the United States of America. This publication is protected by copyright, and permission should be obtained from the publisher prior to any prohibited reproduction, storage in a retrieval system, or transmission in any form or by any means, electronic, mechanical, photocopying, recording, or likewise. For information regarding permissions, write to Pearson Curriculum Rights & Permissions, One Lake Street, Upper Saddle River, New Jersey 07458.

Pearson® is a trademark, in the U.S. and/or in other countries, of Pearson plc or its affiliates.

Scott Foresman® is a trademark, in the U.S. and/or in other countries, of Pearson Education, Inc., or its affiliates.

3 4 5 6 7 V0N4 17 16 15 14 13 12 11 10

Chapter 1 Summer Boredom

Four friends lay on their backs in the tall grass of Trevor's backyard. It was such a sunny day that Jess put on her sunglasses. Ben pulled his baseball cap down over his face, while Trevor and Mario shaded their eyes with their arms.

"So, what do you want to do this summer?" asked Trevor.

"I don't know," Mario sighed.

Jess glanced at her daily planner. "It's been summer for two days," she said. "You can't be bored already."

"I'm bored," Mario said.

"Read a book," Jess said. She handed Mario her copy of Shakespeare's plays. "That will fix you up."

"Sure, if by fix me up you mean make me even more bored," said Mario.

"So, what do you want to do this summer?" Trevor asked again.

"What is there to do in a small town like Greenville in summer?" wondered Mario.

The truth was, there was nothing to do. They had spent many summers in their hometown, and none of them could remember ever doing much at all.

3

"I guess I'll ride my bike," said Mario.

"I guess I'll read," Jess said. "I'm hoping to finish the complete works of William Shakespeare by August. I'm starting with *A Midsummer Night's Dream.*"

The three boys rolled their eyes. Even during summer vacation, Jess couldn't stop reading!

Suddenly, there was a crash inside Trevor's house. It was followed by the panicked voice of his mother and an explosion of giggling from Trevor's three sisters.

"All I know is, I'm going to stay out of the path of Linny, Lizzy, and Lily," he said. "The triplets turned six last week. They are a nightmare times three."

Ben lifted his ball cap off his face. "I want to go to Italy. That's what I want to do this summer."

Trevor looked surprised. "Really?" he said. "Are you going? Why didn't you tell us?"

"Of course I'm not *really* going," said Ben.

"Oh." They all looked a bit deflated at his admission.

"You asked what we wanted to do this summer," said Ben. "That's what I want to do. I want to go to Italy, because I want to eat Italian food. I hear they have the world's best food there."

They all lay quietly for a minute in the tall grass of Trevor's backyard.

"You know, now that you mention it," Mario said, "I'd really like to go to France."

Jess raised her eyebrows. "Why are you so interested in France?" she asked.

"It's where they hold the Tour de France," Mario said.

Jess sniffed. "You mean that bike race where they all wear yellow?"

"They don't all wear yellow," said Mario. "Only the leader wears yellow!"

"Personally," Jess said, "I'd love to go to New York. I've always dreamed of seeing a show on Broadway."

"What about you, Trev? Where do you want to go?" asked Ben.

Trevor sighed. "I would love to go to Topeka."

The others gave Trevor a strange look.

"Topeka?" said Mario. "Topeka, *Kansas*?"

"What's wrong with Topeka?" Trevor asked.

"Nothing, I guess," Mario answered.

"Well, but it's not Italy or France or New York," Jess said. "I would expect Topeka to be a lot like . . . well, a lot like it is here."

"Boring, in other words," said Mario.

"My grandparents live in Topeka," Trevor explained, "and they're definitely not boring. They always have interesting things to talk about. They don't go giggling and screeching after the triplets like all of my other relatives. I miss them."

Ben rolled onto his stomach to get a better look at Trevor. "This is the first time I've heard you mention your grandparents, Trev," he said. "When did you last see them?"

"Six years ago," Trevor said. "We drove down to Topeka. But I don't think we can do that this summer. Now it's all about the triplets and how we need to buy three little pairs of sneakers, three sets of swimming lessons, and three school wardrobes. You get the idea."

"Yeah," Mario said. "Well, if it's any comfort, none of us can afford to go where we want to go, either. We're all going to be stuck right here for the entire summer."

They all sighed collectively at this.

"I have to go," Ben said. "I promised my brother and sister I'd take them to the playground."

They all said their good-byes to Ben, and he ran home. The rest of them lay quietly in the grass.

They stared up at the sky in silence for a long while. Then Mario cleared his throat.

"You know," Mario said, "I'm Italian."

"What has that got to do with anything?" Jess asked, lifting herself up on her elbows.

"Well, my Mom cooks a lot of Italian food at home," Mario answered. "She has some really great dishes that have been passed down in my family. My brothers and I help her out all the time. I could probably make some of her recipes on my own."

Trevor sat up. "What do you mean?"

"Well," said Mario, "I've been thinking. Ben wants to go to Italy so he can try the food. But I could cook him a real Italian meal with dessert and everything. And I think he would like that."

"You know, that's a really nice idea," Jess said.

"Ben *would* like that," said Trevor. "I'm sure of it."

"Do you want help?" Jess asked. "We could make a group activity out of it."

"I know absolutely nothing about Italian cooking," Trevor said, "but I could learn."

"I could help you organize the whole thing," Jess said. "I could make a list and help with the grocery shopping, and I could help make sure you weren't forgetting anything."

Mario raised his eyebrows at Jess.

"Oh! Not that I would expect you to forget anything," she said, blushing.

"Of course not," said Mario, and smiled.

"Perfect!" Trevor said, clapping his hands together. "This is going to be great. Jess, get out your planner. Let's get to work!"

Chapter 2 The Dress Rehearsal

The next week, Jess, Mario, and Trevor were practicing their recipes in Mario's kitchen. Mario and Trevor looked like they had been swimming in tomato sauce, and Jess was covered in flour.

"Is the mozzarella ready?" she called out.

Mario thrust the mozzarella and tomato salad into her hands and swung back to the counter. He threw a meatball into the frying pan, which sat sizzling on the stovetop. Trevor flipped a couple of meatballs from the pan into the big pot that was simmering on another burner.

Mario's mother popped her head into the kitchen. "How's it going?" she asked.

"Everything is under control," Mario and Trevor announced together, as if on cue.

"It smells delicious, kids," she said. "Just give a yell if you need me."

"How are the meatballs?" Jess asked, eyeing her friends. "Did any of the sauce make it into the pot?"

"It's all under control," said Mario, as he threw Trevor a few more meatballs.

"What about the cheesecake—have you decorated it with the fruit yet? Is the bread sliced? Did you grate the Parmesan cheese?"

"Jess!" Mario turned around. He brandished a wooden spoon. "Everything is under control!"

"Well, so you tell me," Jess said. "But, according to my schedule, the cheesecake needs to be cooling while the sauce simmers. We have to get the dress rehearsal right, or the real dinner will be a disaster."

Mario waved the wooden spoon around. "This is not a series of scheduled events!" he said, slightly annoyed. "This is art! I am the artist! The meal flows out of my inspiration! I don't need you to remind me of every little step!"

"Okay then, Trevor," Jess said. "Will you remind the artist to grate the cheese?"

Mario scowled. Trevor was overcome by a violent fit of coughing that seemed suspiciously like an attempt not to laugh.

"I'll get out of your way," Jess said.

"Here." Before she could escape, Mario handed her the cheese, the cheese grater, and a bowl. "Take this with you."

Jess left the kitchen, and Mario leaned on the counter. He wiped his forehead. "Whew!"

Trevor flipped another meatball into the big pot of sauce. "Are you OK?"

"I don't know how my mother does it," Mario said. "I feel like I'm in the middle of a tornado. I can't even remember what things I've done and what things I still have to do. How does a person ever get accustomed to making such big meals?"

"I thought it all flowed from your inspiration," Trevor teased.

Mario snorted. "Yeah, whatever. Thank goodness Jess made me this list, or I wouldn't have the slightest idea what to do next."

"I heard that!" Jess called from the other room. She stuck her head into the kitchen to reassure him. "Don't worry, Mario. You're doing a wonderful job."

The best thing about the dress rehearsal dinner was eating it afterward. Mario and Trevor were exhausted and still covered with sauce, but the meal was delicious! Mario's mother, father, and four brothers were impressed.

"You won't have to cook for this many people the night you have Ben over," his mother said. "I'll be around while you're doing the cooking, and then your father and I will stay in the living room so that the four of you can have your meal in peace."

She ruffled Mario's hair.

"It's going to be spectacular," she said. "You have the touch, Mario. You should make dinner more often."

Mario moaned. "Great." But then he smiled. "Well, I think we're ready to treat Ben to an authentic Italian meal!"

Chapter 3 Ben's Italian Surprise

Ben was a bit relieved when Mario asked him over to dinner. He hadn't seen much of his three best friends lately. Whenever he called, they gave him the oddest excuses for declining his invitations. Jess always seemed to be grocery shopping, while Trevor was forever researching cheeses. And Mario was likely to be sitting at the kitchen table watching bread rise. It all seemed a little suspicious, so Ben had begun to wonder if they didn't like him anymore.

Ben climbed up Mario's steps and knocked on the door. Before he even finished knocking, the door swung open. Jess stood on the threshold.

"*Sorpresa!*" she yelled.

"Huh?" said Ben.

"*Sorpresa!* That's Italian for surprise!"

His friends really had gotten strange lately. "Why are you yelling at me in Italian?"

"Oh, just come in," she said, and pulled him through the door.

An enormous green, white, and red Italian flag hung in the doorway to the kitchen. Streamers in the same colors hung from the family room ceiling and covered the furniture. A woman was singing Italian opera on the stereo.

"I see that Mario's parents have changed the décor," Ben said. He turned in circles, not sure whether to sit on an armchair piled with streamers or stay where he was.

Jess giggled. "Just come into the kitchen," she said. "Soon it will all make sense."

She pushed the flag aside and pulled him through the doorway. Mario and Trevor stood in front of the counter, wearing aprons splattered with red. Trevor was grating cheese, and Mario was piling strawberries and blueberries onto a gigantic cheesecake. Freshly baked bread sat on the counter, while pots bubbled on the stove. The room smelled wonderful, and Ben's mouth watered.

"Hey," Ben said. "What's going on here, guys?"

Mario and Trevor turned toward him. "*Buon giorno!*" Mario said.

"Huh?"

"*Buon giornio*," said Mario again. "It's an Italian greeting."

"I have no idea what's going on here," Ben said, "but it smells so good in this kitchen that I wish I could stay here forever."

Mario, Trevor, and Jess grinned at each other. "Why don't you tell Ben what's going on, Mario?" Jess said.

"You know how you said you wanted to go to Italy to eat Italian food?" he said. "Well, that's what we did."

Ben was shocked. "You went to Italy?"

"Good grief, no," said Mario. "We decided to make an Italian dinner for you."

Ben was so surprised that all he could do was stare at his friends and the heaping piles of food all over the countertops. Grocery shopping. Cheese research. Watching bread rise. Suddenly it all came together. He moved around the room, taking in the sights and scents of all the wonderful food his friends had prepared.

Jess, Mario, and Trevor stood in the middle of the kitchen holding their breath. They weren't sure if Ben liked his surprise or not.

"I can't believe you did this," Ben said, turning back to them. "This is the nicest thing anyone has ever done for me!"

"Whew," said Mario. "You scared us when you just stared like that."

"So, when can we eat?" Ben asked. The three of them burst out laughing.

Ben helped put the finishing touches on the food and carry it all to the table. Then they all sat down together and dug in. They ate, talked, and joked. They told Ben all about how they had planned his Italian surprise. Jess told him all about her lists, and Trevor gave a detailed report of his cheese research. Ben listened intently, but he couldn't really talk because his mouth was constantly full.

"This is the best meal I've ever had," Ben said, as he helped himself to thirds.

Mario's mother was right. The dinner was spectacular.

Chapter 4 Jess Has an Idea

The next day, Jess, Trevor, and Ben sat on a bench in the playground, watching Ben's little brother and sister slide down the slide over and over again.

"You know," Jess said, "I've been thinking."

"What have you been thinking?" asked Ben.

"Well," Jess said, "you know how Mario wanted to go to France to watch the Tour de France?"

"Oh yeah, the race with the yellow shirts," Trevor said.

"Yeah. Well, I've been thinking that it might be nice to do something for Mario, since he can't go to France to see the Tour de France."

"Hey, that's a good idea," said Ben. "What did you have in mind?"

Jess tilted her head and considered. "I wonder if we could arrange a bike race in town?"

"I don't know," Trevor said. "That sounds like a big project that would take an awful lot of organization."

Ben scratched his chin. "If only one of us were organized," he said. He shot Jess a keen smile.

"It would be a challenge," Jess said. "But it would be fun too."

Trevor groaned. "Here we go again."

"Oh, come on, Trev. I can't do it all alone," said Jess. "Besides, I'll bet it will be just as much fun as the dinner!"

Trevor sighed. "Well, do any of you know anything about the Tour de France?"

"Not really," Ben said, shrugging his shoulders.

"I don't know anything about it, either," said Trevor. "But I guess I could look into it. I liked researching those cheeses, and it should be fun to research the race."

"That's a start!" Jess said. "We want it to be as much like the Tour de France as possible." She pulled out her planner. "I'm going to have to contact a lot of people about this. First, we'll need to get permission from the town. I bet we'll need some type of permit. Then maybe we can get the police to help too.

"Oh!" She looked up, excited. "Maybe people can pay to ride, to benefit a charity! What kind of charity would Mario want to support?"

"Well, how about a food bank, or maybe an after-school program," Ben suggested.

"Oh man, this is getting out of hand. We can't possibly organize all of that!" said Trevor.

"Don't be silly. It'll be fun!" Jess chewed on her pen and stared at the sky. "We'll call it the Tour de Greenville."

"The Tour de Greenville," Trevor mused. "Well, this is going to be very interesting."

"The Tour de Greenville," Ben said. "I like it!"

When Jess, Trevor, and Ben met at the ice cream parlor a few days later, they had already made progress.

"Here's what I've learned about the Tour de France," Trevor said. "First off, it lasts three weeks. Jess, please tell me that the Tour de Greenville is not going to last that long."

"Oh dear," Jess said. "Definitely not. I think we had better stick to one day."

"It's also more than two thousand miles long," Trevor said. "It requires agonizing feats of endurance."

"Oh my," Jess said. "We don't want Mario to be exhausted."

"It has stages that take place on flat land and stages that take place in the mountains," Trevor said.

"Well, we don't have any mountains," Jess said, "but we certainly have plenty of flat land."

"Every team starts out with nine riders—"

"Wow," Jess said, "I never realized that this was going to be so complicated. What about the yellow shirt—did you learn anything about the yellow shirt?"

"Oh, yeah. Every day, the person who's winning the race wears the yellow jersey," Trevor said. "The person who wins the whole race wins the yellow jersey. There's also a white jersey, a polka-dotted jersey, a green jersey—"

"Let's keep it simple," Jess said. "Let's have one race that isn't very long. It'll be for kids, and the winner wins a yellow T-shirt that says 'Tour de Greenville.'"

"That sounds pretty manageable," Trevor said.

"Have you talked to anyone yet about the race, Jess?" Ben asked.

"I talked to the police," Jess said, "and the food bank. If we hold the race as a fund-raiser, the food bank can ask the police to block off a few roads for part of the day."

"The food bank," Ben said. "That was a good idea."

"It seemed to make sense," said Jess. "Since Mario likes to cook, he might like that the bike race will help people who can't make their own meals."

"Isn't this going to be a ton of work?" Trevor asked. He hadn't expected to do this much on his summer vacation.

Jess nodded. "It'll be a lot of work," she said, "but it helps to have the police and the food bank working on it too. Now all we really have to do is get the word out."

She turned to Ben. "Can you help with that, Ben? Everyone likes you. Do you think you could mention this to everyone you can think of? We can't have a race without contestants."

"Yeah, I can spread the word," said Ben.

"Say," Trevor said, "how are you going to keep this a secret from Mario?"

"It isn't going to be a secret," Jess said. "We need to tell him right away, because he needs to start training."

17

Chapter 5 The Tour de Greenville

Mario trained intensively for weeks before the race. Ben helped him, riding beside him and cheering him on. The race route wound for five miles through the side streets of their town. Mario had studied it closely so that he could memorize the potholes and learn all the tricky corners.

The night before the race, he oiled his bicycle chain and pumped his tires full of air. He ate a big dinner and went to bed early.

The morning of the Tour de Greenville, Mario awoke fresh and rested. He pulled on shorts and his lucky T-shirt. He rummaged around for his bicycle helmet and headed out to the starting line. Mario was ready.

Jess, Trevor, and Ben weren't riding in the race. Their presence was needed elsewhere; there was just too much organizing to do. Trevor was responsible for signing all of the participants in, making sure everyone had a helmet, and collecting contributions for the food bank. Ben's job was to mingle with the riders and answer their questions. Jess was the busiest of all. She ran back and forth between the police and the volunteers, making sure everyone was in the right place and knew what to do.

At every mile marker, volunteers were supposed to pass out water. At every intersection, volunteers had flags to wave bicyclists in the right direction. There were even people with air pumps and wrenches to help make any necessary last-minute adjustments to the riders' bikes.

When the race began, things only got crazier for Jess. One of the riders fell; one of the volunteers had a megaphone that didn't work; and one of the water stations ran out of water. She darted from one place to another, answering questions and solving problems.

Then somehow, in all of the madness, she misplaced the yellow T-shirt. She looked all around. She raced back to all the places she had been, searching frantically. She asked everyone she ran into if they had seen the shirt.

"Have you seen the yellow T-shirt? Have you seen the yellow T-shirt?" she yelled to Trevor, who sat at a table, shuffling through a pile of registration forms. He stared at her blankly. He pointed to the back pocket of her jeans. Jess reached around and pulled the shirt from her pocket just as she remembered that she had put it there for safekeeping.

Jess blushed. "Don't tell anyone about this," she said.

"I won't," said Trevor. "But you'd better get yourself to the finish line! The first cyclists must be getting close to crossing it."

"Oh no!" said Jess. "I completely forgot that I had to be at the *end* of the race! I'll never get there in time!"

Trevor pointed to Ben's bike and helmet, which leaned against the table.

Jess leaped onto Ben's bike and screeched across the pavement. She cut through driveways and parks, narrowly avoiding flower gardens, until she flew onto the track. When people started cheering, she looked behind her and realized that she was beating the racers. She crossed the finish line and the crowd roared. Mario came in just behind her.

The crowd cheered wildly for Jess.

"No," she cried, "you don't understand! I'm the race organizer!" She pointed to Mario. "He's your winner!"

The crowd applauded Mario. Jess was relieved, and so was Mario.

Jess gave Mario a big hug. "You did it!" she said.

"I couldn't have done it without you!" he said.

Jess wiped her forehead. She had done it. She had organized the very first Tour de Greenville.

Jess presented Mario with the winner's yellow T-shirt. Jess, Mario, Ben, and Trevor had their picture taken by a photographer from the local newspaper. When the hubbub died down, the four friends walked home together.

"What are you going to do next, Jess?" Mario asked. "Run for mayor?"

Jess laughed. "To be honest," she said, "I think I'm going to savor doing nothing for the rest of the summer!"

Chapter 6 Trevor Does More Research

Jess was so tired that she went home early to go to bed, while the boys decided to hang out at Trevor's house for a while.

"That was a great race," said Mario. "You know, we really should do something for Jess to thank her for all she's done."

"Well, you know how she wanted to go to New York to see a Broadway show?" asked Trevor.

"Yes," Mario said. "We know."

They sat quietly for a bit under an oak tree.

Ben raised his eyebrows at Mario. "Any particular reason for asking that, Trev?"

"Well, have you ever wanted to act?" continued Trevor.

"Wait, you mean you want us to put on a play?" Ben said. "For Jess?"

"Sure. After all, Ben got his Italian dinner and Mario got his bike race. I think it would be neat if Jess got her Broadway show," said Trevor.

"Well," said Ben, "I'm not sure we can put on a show like the ones on Broadway."

"Maybe not," said Mario. "But I bet we can come close!"

"Actually," Trevor said, "I've been doing some research. I don't think we could do a whole play, not with only the three of us, but we could put on a sort of mini-play. I was thinking we could do a shortened version of *A Midsummer Night's Dream*. It could be our own special version, with only the most important parts."

"What's that play about?" Mario asked.

"Well, I've been looking into that too," said Trevor. "There's this girl, see, and she's really sad because the guy she loves has a crush on her best friend. Meanwhile, her best friend already has a boyfriend that her father doesn't like very much."

Mario grimaced. "Ugh. It sounds terrible."

"It has some practical jokes in it," Trevor explained. "I figured that you would like to be involved in that, Mario. And I thought you would make a good Oberon, Ben. He's the fairy king."

Mario had to admit that practical jokes sounded appealing. And Ben thought it might be fun to pretend to be a king. But they still needed a few more actors. Mario thought that his brothers might be interested, and Trevor said that they could throw in the triplets if they had to.

"I have a lot more research to do," said Trevor, "but I think Jess would like it. What do you guys think? *A Midsummer Night's Dream: The Short Version*?"

Ben grinned. "It has potential," he said. "It definitely has potential."

"One question, though," said Mario, looking a bit uncomfortable. "Who do we get to play the girls?"

Chapter 7 A Midsummer Night's Dream: The Short Version

A couple of weeks later, Trevor called Jess and asked her to come over. He told her that she was in for a surprise. Jess wasn't sure what to make of this. She hoped that he wasn't going to ask her to organize anything else, because she was still recovering from the bike race.

When she got to his house, Trevor was nowhere to be seen. Either Linny, Lizzy, or Lily let her in, she wasn't sure which one. The girl was wrapped in a sheet and had a dandelion behind her ear. She pulled Jess through the door and had her sit in an armchair, unaccompanied, in the middle of the family room. The chair faced a wall. A doorway to the left of the wall led to the stairs. A doorway to the right of the wall led to the kitchen.

Jess heard rustling and then a giggle. "Where's Trevor?" she asked. The triplet—she still couldn't tell which one—ran through one of the doorways without answering, leaving Jess alone.

Just then Trevor emerged from the right-hand doorway and walked to the center of the wall.

23

"There you are, Trevor," Jess said. "I was beginning to wonder what was going on here." Then she noticed that Trevor was wrapped in a sheet with a length of rope tied around his waist and wore a wreath of fake leaves on his head. He had a very dramatic look on his face.

"Good afternoon, madam," Trevor said, "and welcome." He bowed in a very dramatic way.

"Um, good afternoon," Jess said. "What is this?"

"I am pleased to welcome you to today's performance of *A Midsummer Night's Dream: The Short Version*," Trevor said, "by Trevor Hart."

Now Jess was starting to understand. "*A Midsummer Night's Dream, the Short Version*?" she said. "By you?"

"Surely you are familiar with the former version of the play, called *A Midsummer Night's Dream*, by William Shakespeare," said Trevor.

"Yes," Jess said, "I am."

"Well," Trevor said, "this is the shortened version, featuring only the best parts."

Jess smiled and settled back into her seat. Trevor disappeared through a doorway and the play began.

Ben and one of the triplets appeared from the doorway on the right. They walked to the center of the wall and faced each other. Both wore sheets over their clothes. Ben raised his hands and said, "The king doth keep his revels here tonight!"

"Haven't you jumped ahead a bit?" Jess interrupted. "Isn't that speech in the second act?"

"This is the shortened version, remember?" Trevor's voice called from the doorway on the left. "And it's rude for the audience to talk during the performance!"

Jess thoroughly enjoyed the play. She clapped for Lizzy and Lily, who played the fairies Peaseblossom and Cobweb very well. They really couldn't pronounce most of the words, least of all their own character's names.

She laughed when Mario and Trevor came out. Each time they appeared, they were playing different characters. She laughed at Mario's brother Angelo, who did a wonderful job as Lysander.

She did not laugh at Ben, since his parts were so serious. But she clapped after all his speeches.

The play ended with a lot of running through the living room as the actors acted out a romp through the forest. Their props were cut from cardboard, and they made everything as dramatic as possible, with many shouts and hollers. When the other characters were all put to sleep by the fairy king, Jess jumped to her feet and clapped. The entire cast came out and took a bow.

"Oh, it was wonderful!" Jess said. "It was the best play I've ever seen! I never realized *A Midsummer Night's Dream* was that funny!"

"We couldn't do much in the way of costumes," said Trevor, "or set design, but we hoped it wouldn't matter too much, considering this was only the shortened version."

"It was absolutely perfect," Jess said.

Trevor, Mario, and Ben unwrapped themselves from their sheets and blankets. "Want to go out in the yard?" Trevor asked.

"First, bring me those sheets, Trevor!" his mother called from upstairs. "I'm making up the bed in the guest room."

Trevor dutifully ran upstairs with the sheets, and then the four friends went outside. They found a sunny place in the long grass and lay down on their backs.

Chapter 8 A Summer Well Spent!

They were lying in the same spot they had lain in at the beginning of the summer, but Jess, Mario, Ben, and Trevor felt different.

"I don't remember a summer ever going by this fast," Jess said. "Can you believe it's only a couple of weeks until school starts up again? I haven't read nearly as much as I planned to."

"It's been a good summer," Mario said, "considering that we spent the entire time here."

"A small town like Greenville isn't so bad, after all," said Ben.

"That's true," Mario said. "The Tour de Greenville was just right. I don't think I would have lasted in France. There are way too many mountains."

"And I don't believe Italian food could taste any better in Italy than it did at your house, Mario," said Ben.

"I don't think any Broadway show could have made me laugh as much as *A Midsummer Night's Dream: The Short Version*," Jess said.

"I wish we could've gotten you to Topeka, Trevor," said Mario wistfully. "You're the only one who didn't get your wish."

"That's okay," Trevor said. "It's been a good summer. I can't complain."

"Yeah," said Mario. "It really has been a good summer. I wasn't bored at all."

Just then a car turned down the decline in Trevor's driveway, but only Ben moved to see who it was. He seemed a little bit fidgety that afternoon.

"I wonder who could be coming to visit your family, Trevor," said Ben.

Trevor sighed. "It'll be one of my triplet-loving relatives," he said. "Just wait, in a minute you'll hear the screeching."

"Are you sure about that?" replied Ben. He was clearly trying to hide a sly smile.

Trevor turned to look at his friend. "What are you up to, Ben?"

Ben didn't answer, but turned his attention back to the driveway. A car door slammed, and then another. Someone moved slowly across the yard. Suddenly, a voice spoke above them.

"Well, Trevor?" The voice was shaky, but warm. "Are we too late for the show?"

Trevor's eyes popped open. His jaw dropped as he recognized his grandmother's voice.

"Grandma!" He jumped up and gave her a hug.

"Land sakes, boy," she said, "you've grown like a weed."

"How did . . . " Trevor said. "When did . . . Why did . . . No one told me—"

Trevor's grandfather came from across the yard. "We thought you would enjoy the surprise," he said. "Which one of you boys is Ben?"

Ben shuffled his feet. "That would be me, sir," he said. "It's nice to meet you."

"Such a nice boy," Grandma said. "Your friend Ben gave us a call, Trevor. Told us how much you wanted to see us. He even convinced us to drive here."

"That boy could sell ice in the Arctic," Grandpa said. He shook Ben's hand, and then he hugged Trevor. "Just look at how tall you are, son."

Trevor's eyes were a little misty. He gulped. "I can't believe it," he said.

"Believe it, boy," said Grandma. "Now, you never answered my question. Did we miss this show of yours? This *A Midsummer Night's Dream, Condensed*, or whatever you call it?"

"*A Midsummer Night's Dream: The Short Version*," Trevor said. "Yes, I'm afraid you did miss it."

"Oh, but you can do it again," Jess said, "can't you?"

"Sure we can," Mario said. "We can do an encore for your grandparents!"

"But my mother took our costumes away to make up the bed in the spare room," Trevor reminded them. "And Angelo left."

"We'll raid the towel closet," Mario said. "Don't worry, we'll think of something."

"I can play Lysander," Jess said.

Trevor's smile stretched from ear to ear, and he hugged his grandparents once more. "Okay," he said. "Let's do it again. *A Midsummer Night's Dream: The Short Version!*"

It was just as good the second time around, even though Trevor grinned through the entire play. He couldn't help it. He was just so happy.

The Tour de France

Mario dreams of seeing the Tour de France, and he is not alone! Every summer, millions of people watch the world's biggest cycling event.

The Tour de France lasts for about three weeks and is 2,235 miles long. In 2005, for the seventh time, American Lance Armstrong won the race. Many people don't realize that cycling is a team sport. Lance could not have won the Tour de France without his excellent team.

If you cycle just behind another rider, then that rider will break the air and help you to expend less energy as you cycle. This is called "drafting."

Lance has a few cyclists on his team who are great climbers. On the hilly parts of the Tour, Lance drafts off his climbers until that climber is too tired to lead anymore. Then Lance takes off by himself.

There are many times when Lance's team only has the energy to take him so far, and then he must continue on by himself. Some parts of the Tour are individual races, in which each rider must ride alone without the help of a team. And Lance does his fair share of the leading. He is such a strong rider that sometimes his entire team drafts behind him!